Etwall Primary School
Egginton Road
Etwall
Derbyshire
DE65 6NB

OXFORD
UNIVERSITY PRESS

Comic Illustrators

Bronwyn Tainui

Contents

- Comic Strips 3
- Rupert Bear and Mary Tourtel 4
- Charles Schulz 8
- Asterix, a Comic Book 14
- Keeping Asterix Alive 20
- Index 24

Comic Strips

An old comic strip from a 1940s newspaper

The Simpsons is a comic strip you can see today. The Simpsons is also a TV cartoon show.

People began to draw comic strips over 100 years ago. This way of telling funny jokes or adventure stories became popular in newspapers. More people will buy a newspaper if it has a good comic strip.

Rupert Bear and Mary Tourtel

Mary Tourtel

character – a person in a story

In 1920, people who worked at the *Daily Express* in Britain wanted more children to look at their newspaper. They needed to find a character that would appeal to children.

Mary Tourtel drew a bear she called Rupert. Children loved him. Rupert has been seen in the comic strip in the *Daily Express* ever since.

cartoon – a funny drawing

Rupert has not changed much over the years. He still wears checked trousers, a sweater and a scarf.

Rupert is an animal cartoon character, but he behaves as though he is human. Rupert is just like a boy.

As well as drawing Rupert, Mary Tourtel wrote the stories of his adventures. She also invented other characters to be his friends.

Mary Tourtel had been trained as an artist. Her **illustrations** of Rupert and his friends showed lots of interesting little details.

Rupert setting off on an adventure

Mary Tourtel's stories about Rupert were like fairy tales. Rupert met knights, princesses and magicians on his adventures.

Mary Tourtel stopped illustrating Rupert in 1930. Since then, other illustrators have drawn the comic strip about the little bear. Since 1935, people have written and illustrated whole books about Rupert, too.

Charles Schulz

A *Peanuts* comic strip from a newspaper.

Charlie Brown is one of the most popular *Peanuts* characters.

Charles Schulz was another famous comic illustrator. He was probably one of the most popular illustrators in the world. He drew comic strips. His comic strips have appeared in over 2300 newspapers. He has also published more than 1400 books.

Characters from the *Peanuts* comic strip

comic – a magazine for children containing comic strips

Charles Schulz

Charles Schulz was born on November 26, 1922 in Minnesota, USA. He was very shy. He drew a lot when he was growing up. But he did not become famous until much later. In 1950, the first ever comic strip of *Peanuts* appeared in a newspaper.

People loved *Peanuts*. One reason they liked it was because it had a lot of characters. Until then, most comic strips only had two or three. The characters included the famous Charlie Brown, Snoopy, Woodstock, Linus, Lucy, Marcie and Schroeder.

Lucy

People also loved *Peanuts* because the characters were so interesting. The friends told the truth to each other in a way that had not been done before. They had feelings and problems like real people. They were very funny, too.

Charlie Brown's friend Linus

Charles Schulz drew *Peanuts* **for 30 years. He always worked by himself. He did the same things every day. First he would eat a muffin with jam, drink some coffee and then start to work at his drawing table. He always used the same pens.**

Charles Schulz never thought he would be so famous and that people would love his work so much.

When he started to earn millions of dollars for his comics, he gave a lot of his money away. He just wanted to live an ordinary life.

Charles Schulz was 77 years old when he finally stopped drawing comic strips about Charlie Brown and his friends.

Asterix, a Comic Book

Albert Uderzo with Asterix at the Asterix theme park

invaders – people who force their way into a country and take it over

Asterix is a comic character who is popular with older children and many teenagers. The Asterix adventures take place in 50 BC, in a seaside village in Gaul, in France. In the story, most of the country has been taken over by the Roman invaders. One small village holds out against the Romans.

colour-blind – unable to see certain colours

Getafix

Albert Uderzo drawing Getafix the Druid

Albert Uderzo draws the funny cartoon illustrations for Asterix. Albert Uderzo was born in France in 1927. Albert's parents knew that their young son had a lot of talent, so he went to art lessons. The teacher found out that Albert was colour-blind. But this did not stop him drawing wonderful cartoons.

translated – changed into another language

René Goscinny was the person who wrote the Asterix adventure stories that Albert Uderzo illustrated. For many years they made a very good team. Their Asterix stories have been translated into nearly 100 languages.

René Goscinny explaining a new idea for a story

Obelix

Obelix and Dogmatix

Albert Uderzo said that the hardest part of creating an Asterix book was getting a good idea for a new story. Albert and René would talk for hours. All sorts of things might spark off a new idea. It might be an object from Asterix's Roman world, or a plan for a new journey Asterix might go on.

René and Albert with Asterix in the snow

Albert with a new Asterix book

When the two men had decided on an idea, René would work on the story first. He wrote a paragraph about 13 lines long, for each page of the book. Each line described a bit of the story. Albert drew a picture to show what happened in each line. Each set of pictures made one page of the book.

18

If Asterix visited another country in a story, Albert would need to take a trip there, too. He took photos to show what it was like. Then he copied the parts of the photographs in his drawings.

19

Asterix is so famous he is even on a French postage stamp.

Keeping Asterix Alive

Sadly, René Goscinny died in 1977. Asterix fans wanted Albert Uderzo to continue with the Asterix stories. He agreed. Albert Uderzo has now become both the writer and illustrator of Asterix.

Albert has found ways to make his illustrations different to other comic strips. He sometimes adds pictures in the speech bubbles, as well as words. He often makes an extra joke by drawing the speech bubbles in funny shapes, or by using funny letters.

Albert draws each panel in pencil first, to make sure everything will fit. He checks that the story is easy to understand from the pictures. Then he draws the picture outlines in ink. Finally, he colours them in.

Nearly all of the characters in Asterix have huge noses, however big or small their bodies are. Albert says this is because many people believe that a person with a big nose is always good-natured. Giving the characters big noses is a way of showing what nice, kind people Asterix and his friends are.

Index

artist 6

character/s 4-6, 8-11, 14, 23

comic/s 3, 4, 7-10, 13, 14, 21

illustrations 6, 15, 21

illustrator/s 7, 8, 16, 20

magicians 7

writer 16, 20